Born to Run

The Story of Brittany Young

By
Barbara Rudow

www.scobre.com

For Taylor and Allison.

Chapter One

The Burn Pit

Brittany Young is a unique sixteen-year-old girl growing up on the island of Maui. This beautiful island is one of the eight that make up Hawaii. It's small enough to drive around in less than a day. Maui has more than 100,000 residents and Brittany considers herself lucky to be one of them.

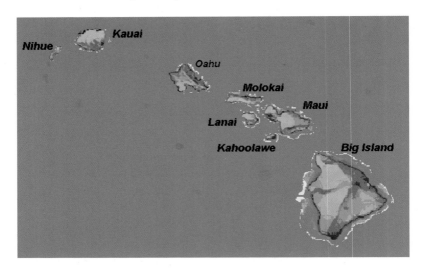

This lively teenager enjoys all that Maui has to offer. She loves to surf, snorkel, paddle, and barbeque at the beach. She also loves Maui's world-famous sunsets. Brittany's college plans will likely take her to mainland America. Still, the spirit of the islands will always be with her.

When you meet Brittany, the first thing you see is a cheerful, easy smile. Her life seems carefree, but she has actually been through some tough times. When Brittany was only seven, her life changed forever . . .

The date was May 24, 1997. It seemed like a normal spring day. Seven-year-old Brittany was returning from a birthday party. The Young family car turned onto Cooke Road. Once there, Brittany, and her brother Jake made their usual request. They wanted to walk the rest of the way home. The Young's lived on a mile-long dusty road. The road was dotted with houses, each hidden behind eucalyptus trees.

Brittany and her brother Jake stand in their front yard.

Mrs. Young pulled over, and Jake jumped out of the car. Brittany was right behind him. Jake was nine, eighteen months older than his sister. The two seemed attached at the hip.

Mrs. Young called out to Brittany. She reminded her daughter to put her shoes on.

"Jake doesn't have shoes on," Brittany argued.

Before Mrs. Young could reply, her two children were off and running. The two of them soon passed an old protea farm. In its day, this farm was beautiful. Protea are one of the world's most unusual flowers. They grow especially well in the Kula area of Upcountry Maui. Kula, where Brittany lived, sits on the side of Haleakala, which is a volcano.

A Protea flower in full blossom.

Jake and Brittany stopped when they reached the old farm. The owner had let most of the flowers die off a while ago. He didn't take care of his land. In fact, a grand old eucalyptus tree used to live on his property. The tree towered over the road. It had been removed a few years earlier, but the giant stump had remained. The owner did not want to pay to have the stump taken out. Instead, he decided to burn it, turning it into a dangerous fire pit.

The stump eventually sank to the earth. When it did, it left behind a crater fourteen feet wide and five feet deep. Jake stared at the hole where the stump had once sat. He moved closer to the crater with Brittany close behind. When they got to the edge, they looked in. They had watched the tree shrink in size for many months. They never really believed it would be gone. But it was.

In the past, they had seen open flames in the stump. The fire had scared them off. Today, the white ash looked like a blanket of snow covering the hole. Jake poked his stick into the circle. The fire appeared to be gone. There was something that they didn't understand, though. Although there were no flames, the coals were still hot beneath the white cover.

Jake and Brittany circled the crater, poking their sticks into the ash. Brittany reminded Jake that they were supposed to go home. Jake told her that they'd go in a minute. Then he stepped onto the inside ledge that lined the pit. It was like taking the first step into a pool. Brittany followed him. Jake made it to the other side of the crater first. Because he had, Brittany was sure that the ground was solid everywhere. But it wasn't.

Brittany put her left foot down onto the ledge. Then, she began to sink. At first she didn't realize what was going on. It happened so quickly. Before she knew it, she had sunk up to her knees. It was then that Brittany began to feel intense heat beneath her feet. There was also a bitter acid taste in her mouth. A moment of stunned silence followed. The birds even seemed to hold their breath. That silence was soon shattered by an endless scream.

Brittany's legs were covered in hot coals. The temperature was around 1200 degrees, quickly destroying Brittany's thin legs. Somehow, she managed to escape. Unable to use her legs, Brittany pushed herself out of the hole with her arms. At this point, she wasn't fully aware of what she was doing. All she could think about was getting home. She could feel her shins burning. Her feet were burning, too.

Then, something amazing happened. She ignored her burning legs—legs that shouldn't have been able to move. (In fact, it would be months before she would even be able to walk again.) Defying logic and science, she ran. She shot up from the burning hole in the ground and sprinted up the road. Skin fell from her legs with every step she took. A person burned this badly, should not have been able to move, let alone run.

Brittany will always remember seeing her "transparent toenails floating in blood." She'll never forget the black rings that had formed beneath her knees. These were the scariest moments of her life.

When she got home, Brittany's feet had swollen to four times their normal size. Her legs didn't even look like legs. Somehow, though, she had made it home. There is no scientific way to explain how she did it.

Brittany's father was outside mowing the lawn. He was stopped cold by his daughter's screams. He turned off the mower and ran toward her. Seeing the damage, he lifted her and hurried toward the house.

When Mrs. Young got to the door, she saw her husband running toward her. Brittany was dangling from his arms. Mrs. Young fought back tears. Then she quickly placed Brittany in the back seat of the car. She alertly remembered her first aid training as she did so. She knew that she had to cool the burns. So she ran towels under cold water and wrapped each of Brittany's legs. This needed to be done, even though it hurt.

In most places, the first thing to do would be to call 911. But the Young home was located on Haleakala. This meant that it was very difficult to get to. It would take a long time for an ambulance to make the trip. They decided to drive the thirty minutes down the mountain and to the hospital.

This photo of Haleakala shows why getting an ambulance to Brittany's home was so difficult.

Brittany sat with her towel-wrapped feet in a cooler of ice. Mr. Young drove. He was trying to go fast, but had to dodge bumps and potholes at the same time. The drive down the mountain, which was usually peaceful, seemed like a nightmare.

When Brittany arrived at Maui Memorial Hospital she was treated immediately. The doctor on call, however, was not experienced with burns. He didn't know how serious Brittany's injuries were. It took the help of a special nurse to recognize Brittany's need for more extensive care. The nurse also gave Brittany a teddy bear. Brittany named him Boo Boo and has him to this day.

After just a few minutes, the medical team decided to have Brittany flown to Honolulu. This is

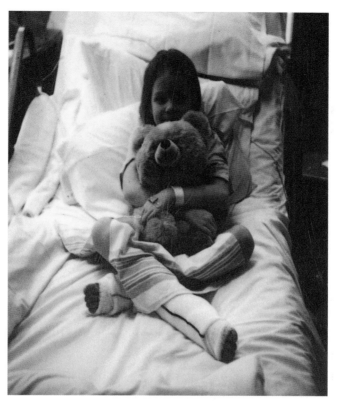

Brittany, in her hospital bed with her teddy bear Boo Boo.

the largest city on the island of Oahu. Honolulu has several hospitals—including a burn center. Without proper care, Brittany's legs might not heal properly. The doctors quickly wheeled her stretcher onto a two-prop plane. They knew that they had to hurry. Every minute would help save Brittany's legs, giving her the chance to walk again.

Besides Brittany and the paramedics, only one person could fit into the plane. This was devastating.

Neither parent wanted to leave Brittany's side. Mrs. Young ended up going with Brittany on the twenty-five minute trip to Oahu. The flight seemed to take about ten times that long.

As the plane soared above the clouds, Brittany lay on the stretcher. She was in great pain. The noisy plane was so loud that she could barely talk. Mrs. Young stared out the window. She was very upset, but tried not to panic.

Her thoughts were interrupted when the pilot announced that they were five minutes from landing. Mrs. Young looked at her daughter and forced a smile. Brittany squeezed her hand and smiled back. She was being strong and brave, but the worst was far from over.

Chapter Two

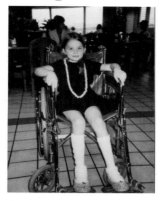

The Road to Recovery

The doctors had bad and good news for Brittany. The bad news was that fifteen percent of her body had been burned. In many spots, the burns were third degree—which was serious. Her feet were the worst. The doctors were afraid that she would lose several toes on her left foot.

The good news was that it was a "clean burn." As it turned out, it was lucky that Brittany hadn't been wearing shoes that day. If she had been, they would have melted into her feet. In that case, things would have been worse. The doctors very likely would have had to amputate.

Dr. Linda Rosen handled Brittany's case. She was a great doctor. Unfortunately, she wasn't a magician and she couldn't make the pain disappear. Dr. Rosen explained to Brittany why she was feeling so much pain. When people are badly burned, the injured area feels as if it is still burning for several days. Only time would heal Brittany's wounds.

Brittany's father made his way to Oahu the following morning. She was happy to see him. Her brother had stayed behind, though. Brittany talked to Jake on the phone from the hospital, but it wasn't the same. She also missed her little sister, Makenna.

The Young family, standing in front of their home in Kula.

As the days passed, Brittany really started to miss her friends at school. Her classmates had sent presents, cards, and balloons. They sent so many that her hospital room looked like a party supply store.

Despite the gifts and phone calls, living in a hospital was no fun. Her body healed slowly. And every day, she had to go through painful procedures and physical therapy. It had been three weeks since her accident and she was *still* unable to walk.

This made her sprint up the hill on Cooke Road twice as amazing. When Mrs. Young told the story, Brittany's doctors were all left scratching their heads. They were confused. How was Brittany able to move like that in the condition her legs were in? What the doctors didn't know was that this girl was special— she was born to run.

As special as Brittany was, her legs were still in serious condition. One of the main issues she faced every day was infection. Burn victims' skin, which protects them, is gone. This makes them more likely to get infections. To fight this, Brittany's bandages were changed two times every day. This was the most painful thing she had to go through during her hospital stay.

Twice every day Brittany would be taken to a soundproof room with giant sinks. Once there, doctors would take off her bandages and place her legs in warm water. Then they would scrub them with gauze for twenty minutes. This removed all the old skin. While they scrubbed, Brittany clenched a Popsicle stick between her teeth. This kept her from screaming. The pain was so terrible that Brittany bit through it every time.

Brittany later described this procedure: "Imagine taking sand paper to a deep cut," she said, "to the muscle or even bone, and rubbing back and forth to try to remove layers of skin. Now imagine that all over your feet and shins."

Brittany welcomed any escape from the pain. She was thrilled when a special visitor showed up. For the first three weeks of her hospital stay, Brittany had been stuck in her room. By the fourth week, the pain had lessened. Brittany was able to sit in a wheelchair and move around a bit. One of her favorite places to go was the playroom.

On this special day, Miss Universe 1997 was coming to visit! When Miss Universe, Brook Mahealani Lee, walked into the room, Brittany was mesmerized. She was wearing a massive, diamond-studded tiara. Later, Brittany got to try it on.

Wearing her diamond-studded tiara, Brittany sits with Miss Universe 1997, Brook Mahealani Lee.

Like Brittany, Miss Universe was from Hawaii. She had come to the hospital to cheer up the young patients. She played cards with Brittany and told her about her travels. Brittany says that her visit was the highlight of her hospital stay.

What Brittany really wanted, though, was to be outside. She was tired of bandage changes and physical therapy. But she knew that although her treatments were very painful, they were very important. She went every day for an hour and refused to cry.

One thing Brittany enjoyed was being able to eat anything she wanted. That's right—anything! Burn victims tend to lose a lot of weight. Their bodies use about 10,000 to 15,000 calories a day to fight the burn. This means they need to eat a lot of food. To maintain her weight, Brittany was able to eat all the candy she wanted! She lived on Rolos. Dr. Rosen walked into Brittany's room some days with cans of whipped cream. She would ask Brittany to eat all of them! Despite the doctors' best efforts, Brittany still lost ten pounds. She was losing weight, but she was also getting better. Still, she wondered if she'd ever see home again.

In late June—six weeks after her accident— Brittany was wheeled out of the hospital. It was a sunny day, and the tropical air was like a taste of heaven. She was finally free!

As she left the hospital, she took a final look around the playroom. She observed the kids around her closely. For over a month, they had all lived together. In that time, Brittany hadn't spent much time thinking about what *they* went through. Naturally, she had focused on her own pain. Now, with the worst behind her, she felt great compassion. She noticed that many of them had no hair because of chemotherapy treatments. Some were so deformed that she couldn't even guess what had caused it. Tears welled up in her eyes.

Even at seven years old, Brittany knew that she was lucky. Sitting in a wheelchair with burned legs and feet wasn't *that* bad. Things could have been much worse.

Brittany was forever changed when she left the hospital. Sure, she was excited to get back to her old life. But she knew that nothing would ever be the same. Especially not the way she looked at the world. She left that day with an inner strength that most people never achieve.

The Shriners Hospital for Children in Honolulu.

Chapter Three

Back in Maui

Being back in Maui didn't mean that Brittany's ordeal was over. She was now able to walk on her own, but she had to move very slowly. The skin on her legs was paper thin. Any contact—even the slightest bump—would cause the skin to fall off. This was extremely painful.

Brittany wasn't able to wear shoes for another four months either. Luckily, her mom found her a pair of oversized, soft-top sandals. These were perfect for Brittany to wear when she went outside. The sandals were funky, striped, and kind of cool. The tops of Brittany's feet were the most tender areas. Because of this, she took extra care of them. Before she slipped into her sandals, she put on a thick sock. This sock went over her Jobst stockings.

Jobst stockings are medical stockings that protect the legs of burn victims. Brittany was forced to wear them for two full years. These stocking were a constant reminder to Brittany—and the world around her—of her accident.

Brittany's activities were limited. Her doctors *did* give her permission to swim, though. Brittany loved the water, so this meant the world to her. The public pool in Pukalani, the neighboring town, was her favorite place. Before her injury, she met her friends there almost every day.

The public pool in Pukalani.

It had been two months since she'd stepped into the burn pit. Brittany hadn't been out of the house much since. This made her anxious to hang out with her friends Hannah and Claire.

In the locker room, Brittany changed into her bathing suit. As she and Hannah made their way to the pool, she gripped Hannah's arm to prevent falling.

Brittany was about to step into the water when a whistle sounded loudly. In front of everyone, the lifeguard called Brittany over. He told her she couldn't swim with her stockings on. It was against the rules. She explained that she couldn't take them off, but he ignored her. The lifeguard refused to let her in the water. Brittany was crushed and totally embarrassed. She headed back to the locker room.

That was the first time Brittany realized that she was different. She was beginning to see that not everyone was going to be understanding. In fact, people could be cruel.

A few months later, Brittany began third grade. At this point, she was able to walk fairly normally. She still went to physical therapy once a week. She also went to The Shriners Hospitals for Children on Oahu every few months. There she was examined and fitted for new Jobst stockings.

Brittany still couldn't do anything too active—like running. She tried not to dwell on it, though. For now, she was just happy to be walking. Of course, when she closed her eyes at night, she would have amazing dreams: she was sprinting down the road, or on the beach—her legs working the way they once had.

Overall, Brittany was proud of the progress she had made. In fact, when asked by her teacher, she agreed to tell her class all about her accident. Standing in front of twenty-five students, she spoke about the fire pit and her burns. That seemed to make her classmates uncomfortable. She quickly shifted gears, focusing on fun things like eating candy and meeting Miss Universe.

When asked what the best part of her ordeal was, Brittany told them about the "recovery" cruise. It was over the summer with Brittany's grandparents. They thought the family needed a break from hospital and physical therapy sessions. The entire family went on a cruise around the Hawaiian islands. Of course, Brittany was limited by her injuries.

Her family got the chance to hike Kilauea, which is a volcano on Hawaii (The Big Island). Kilauea had recently erupted, so they were able to see lava flowing down the mountain into the ocean. It was awesome! Brittany wasn't able to walk on the rocky ground. She didn't miss out though. Her mother carried her on her back so she could see everything up close.

Mount Kilauea . . . erupting!

When her classmates asked Brittany what the *worst* part of her ordeal was, she made a joke. She told them how mad she was when the doctors cut off her favorite shorts. After everyone stopped laughing, a boy asked if he could see her legs.

At this question, Brittany paused. She *was* proud of the progress she had made in her recovery. But she also knew that there was some scarring. Her left foot— the first foot to slip into the pit—was the worst. To fix this, doctors had suggested grafting.

Grafting is a surgical procedure where doctors transplant living tissue to replace other, damaged tissue. For Brittany, this would have meant taking skin from her buttocks. After cutting a patch of skin, they would move it to her feet. It would have been very painful and would have left a scar on her buttocks. If one thing went wrong, they would have to start over again. After a great deal of thought, she and her parents decided against it.

She thought about this decision while the class leaned in closer to check out her legs. Brittany slowly unwrapped the bandages. Once exposed, most of the kids stared—but they were very nice about it.

The boy who had asked to see it, however, right away yelled out, *"Ugh, that's gross!"*

Brittany quickly covered up. She hadn't considered how her legs looked to others. To her, the scarring was no big deal. After all, she remembered the kids at The Shriners Hospital. They had serious—

life threatening—burns and illnesses. Compared to theirs, her scars were minor. It had never occurred to her that someone would look at her injuries and be grossed out. Brittany felt ashamed and sad. She also felt more determined than ever to get better.

She followed doctor's orders and didn't do any activity that she wasn't supposed to. The thing she needed most was time. The skin needed to heal. As frustrating as that was, there was nothing she could do about it.

Two years later, by fifth grade, Brittany considered herself healed. She still had to go to the hospital in Oahu twice a year, but her therapy was complete. She no longer needed to wear the hot, itchy Jobst stockings. This thrilled her, of course! So did the next piece of news. She was given the go-ahead to play whatever sports she wanted. One of her favorite activities was hiking.

On Maui, many hiking trails lead to beautiful waterfalls like this one.

Brittany's first real athletic experience was the Kula Elementary School's Annual Fun Run. This fundraiser was an event in which students raced twice around the playing fields at school. Brittany hadn't run it since the first grade, so she was very excited about the race.

By race time, she was bouncing with excited energy. Still, she didn't have any expectations of winning. She was just glad to be participating. When the whistle blew, Brittany exploded out front. She wasn't even breathing hard as she finished her first lap. There was a huge smile on her face. She felt strong as her unbandaged legs pumped hard through each stride.

Running was the most amazing feeling in the world! Her ponytail whipped back as she sprinted. The rush she felt was awesome. She picked up speed as she made her way around the fields during her second and final lap. Honestly, she didn't want the run to end. If nobody was around, she would have happily run a third lap.

Brittany was close to the finish line when she realized that her friend Lindsay was a few strides behind her. The rest of the kids were much farther back. Lindsay had won this event the past few years. This year, she assumed that she would win it again. Brittany knew that winning meant a lot to Lindsay— more than it did to Brittany. Nobody expected Lindsay to get beaten. *Especially* not by a girl who only a short while ago was not even able to walk!

Brittany was easily in first place when she started to slow down. Finally, she stopped, waiting for her friend to catch up. The two girls crossed the finish line together a few strides later. For Brittany, this race wasn't about finishing first. In her eyes, she had won the moment she started to run.

Chapter Four

Who's Got Spirit?

The following fall, Brittany began middle school. She was having no pain in her legs or feet at this point. Still, she had to go to Oahu twice a year for check-ups. The scarring was going to be permanent, but Brittany had accepted that.

When Brittany was twelve, she celebrated her recovery by learning the sport of the ancient Hawaiians—surfing. Maui boasts some of the best surf spots in the world. Brittany, because of her burns, had never been able to experience them. She was so excited by this new sport that she surfed nearly every weekend. She went down to Puamana Park or Launiupoko. These are two of the most popular surf spots on the west side of Maui.

Brittany loved the challenge of catching a wave on her board. She also loved the peaceful side of surfing. Sometimes, she would sit quietly on her board

Brittany and her father standing beside her new surf board.

waiting for the next set of waves. If she was lucky, green sea turtles would be swimming nearby. In the winter, she would look out and see the humpback whales—regular visitors to the waters off Maui. These were some of her favorite times on her board.

The humpback whales travel to Hawaii every year from their feeding grounds in the Arctic Ocean off Alaska. To mark the arrival of winter on the mainland, people look for the first sign of snow. On Maui, people look for the first whale, which usually arrives in mid-November. They are always spectacular to see.

Aside from surfing, most of Brittany's activities centered around her school. Brittany attended Seabury Hall, an independent college preparatory school for grades six through twelve. The school looms one mile above Makawao Town. The view peeks down on Maui's North Shore and the West Maui Mountains and then onto the expansive blue ocean.

Brittany balanced her studies with lots of extracurricular activities. She starred in school plays (she was an elf in *The Hobbit* and a pirate in *Treasure Island*), played sports, and served on school committees. But her favorite thing in middle school was being part of the spirit committee.

The spirit committee helps get students involved and enthusiastic about school activities. Brittany's loved Spirit Week the most. During spirit week, the spirit committee picks a different theme each day. All the students then dress accordingly. There are crazy hair days, superhero days, 1970s days, and even pirate days.

Another one of Brittany's favorite school activities is the Winterim program. Brittany's eighth-grade Winterim was her favorite. Winterim is a four-day trip where students explore many areas of interest.

Brittany is very interested in the study of nature. So the Winterim course she chose was a hike into the Haleakala Crater. It takes about an hour to drive from Brittany's home up to the top of Haleakala. Hiking down into the crater itself, though, takes much longer. The crater is very steep, and the hike is strenuous. Brittany's legs and feet were now strong enough to make this multiday trip. There are very few people in the world who have hiked into the crater of a volcano. Brittany is one of them.

Brittany, center, during her Winterim adventure into Haleakala Crater.

Haleakala, which means "house of the sun," is a dormant volcano that last erupted in 1790. It is 10,000 feet high. The crater is 3,000 feet deep and is large enough to hold the entire island of Manhattan! The Seabury Winterim group spent three nights in cabins spread inside of the crater. They saw native plants, such as the Haleakala Silversword (Ahinahina), which is part of the sunflower family. Haleakala is the only place on the planet where this unique flower is found.

Haleakala Silversword in full bloom.

Brittany had a great time hiking and learning about Haleakala. Just like surfing, the quiet times were what she loved most. One night, a few kids decided to sleep outside. Brittany was a member of this adventurous group. She lay in her sleeping bag, trying to stay warm. Brittany fell asleep stargazing. She woke with frost on her sleeping bag. The beauty of the morning made her think of an old Maui expression: "Maui No Ka Oi," which means "Maui is the best."

Brittany and her friends, Jazzy and Erin, return to Haleakala Crater a few years later. They huddle up to stay warm just after sunrise.

The Seabury sports clubs also played a major role in Brittany's life. She had fallen behind athletically because of years of inactivity. This didn't discourage her, though. Instead, she worked twice as hard to catch up.

The middle school sports schedule is divided into quarters. This allowed Brittany to do cross country, volleyball, basketball, and track. The two running clubs quickly became her favorites. They were also the clubs that would have a major impact on Brittany's future.

When Brittany started cross country, she had never run longer than a short sprint. She was not prepared for the strength and will it took to be successful in cross country. In fact, her first race in the sixth grade was a disaster. She finished the 1½ mile race but was almost dead last. She never placed that season, but she never quit.

Brittany and her middle school cross country team.

Aside from being a determined person, Brittany was motivated to help her team win. In cross country, the first five runners for each team receive points based on the position they place. During her seventh-grade season, Brittany set a goal—to win at least one ribbon. When you place in the top ten you win a ribbon. Not surprisingly, she accomplished this easily. She soon started closing the gap between her and the competition, though never placing better than seventh.

By eighth grade, Brittany had won several second place ribbons. She still hadn't finished first, though. The Seabury team certainly did. In fact, they took first place in the league.

Brittany was starting to like long distance running. Still, her heart was on the track . . . or, in Brittany's case, on the soccer field. That's because Seabury Hall does not actually have a track. They paint white stripes on a soccer field for lanes and finish lines. These conditions didn't discourage Brittany. She loved running there.

Although Brittany only ran in certain events, she made sure to watch all of them. She is a natural team leader, always encouraging. Yes, she wanted to win herself. She was also happy to just be out there. After going through what she had, running was enough. Winning was the icing on the cake.

By the end of eighth grade, Brittany's injury was well behind her. She had turned a page in her life. After seven long years of rehab, treatment, and check-ups, it was finally over. She no longer had to go to The Shriners Hospitals for checkups. Truthfully, Brittany had mixed emotions. She had been flying over to Oahu since the second grade. Sure, she was thrilled to be considered healed, but she would miss the friends she'd made there.

For the rest of her life, these memories will be a source of inspiration. Her accident is a constant reminder of how lucky she is to be alive. Now, thoughts of those less fortunate drive her to continue running when everything in her body is telling her to stop.

Totally exhausted after a run.

Chapter Five

Pies, Pies, Pies

The 2003 cross country season was Brittany's introduction to high school running. She went through some amazing physical changes that year, too. A growth spurt made her stronger, faster, and able to run longer without tiring. These changes seemed to take place overnight. When she hit the trails her freshman year, she knew that something had clicked for her.

Brittany's freshman cross country season was highlighted by the return of Tia Ferguson. Tia had moved to the mainland a year earlier. She had returned to Seabury Hall for her senior year. Tia was a state champion in several events.

In chasing Tia, Brittany improved dramatically. In fact, she ran well enough to qualify for the state meet. Although she did not place, she received a special honor: she made the Maui Interscholastic League (MIL) All-Stars. This is awarded to the top ten runners in Maui. Brittany was proud of this accomplishment. She was one of just two freshmen on the team. Running alongside older and more experienced girls helped her learn what it took to succeed in this sport.

That spring, Brittany got on a real track for the first time. This took place under the direction of the Seabury track coach, Rudy Huber. During the fall cross country season, Brittany had learned how to compete. Now she was ready to apply her new skills on the track. Coach Rudy noticed Brittany's potential right away. He decided to have her run the four hundred meter dash in the first meet of the season. Brittany had never run this race before. In fact, she had never run on a track before.

She lined up next to the other runners. The hard ground beneath her feet felt strange. She had no idea how fast or slow she would be on this new surface. Her feet gripped the ground and she took a deep breath. The gun sounded and Brittany took off like a rocket. After just a few strides, she was well ahead of the pack. In those first few steps, it was clear that Brittany was a serious competitor. She ran the race in 63 seconds. This time qualified her for the state meet— after her first race ever on a track!

That race cemented in Brittany's mind that she

was going to be a "runner." Until then, Brittany had raced with little training. Now, she was running to win. She made that very clear during the MIL finals. Brittany ran the 400 meter dash in 59.02 seconds. This time shattered a 24-year-old record. Her record-setting time still holds today!

Once Brittany started winning races, she didn't stop.

During her freshman track season, Brittany ran nearly every race: the one hundred, two hundred, four hundred, eight hundred, fifteen hundred, three thousand, and even the long jump. She placed fourth in the state meet in the four hundred meter dash. Although she was only fourteen, people in the Maui track world were starting to talk about her.

Coach Rudy was interviewed about Brittany in the Maui News: "Brittany has that drive, she's a special athlete," he said. "She's probably the most versatile runner in the state. She's the only runner I know who can run a 13.1 in the one hundred and go all the way up to the three thousand."

Despite her success on the track, Brittany stayed involved in other sports. She was unwilling to focus on just one activity. The high school sports program was set up in trimesters. This allowed Brittany to play soccer during the second trimester, between cross country and track. She thought it would be fun, as well as a good way to stay in shape. What she lacked in soccer skills, she made up for with determination and speed. That is how she was able to play varsity soccer as a freshman.

Aside from sports, Brittany spent much of ninth grade babysitting and baking pies. She baked lots and lots of pies. In recovering from her burns, Brittany had been forced to stay inside a lot. During that time, she taught herself how to bake. The Young family had fruit trees on their property that Brittany used for her pies. She especially loved the apples and white peaches.

Being a great baker came in handy during the end of her freshman year. Brittany's Spanish teacher was planning to take a group of students to Spain that summer. Brittany wanted to go more than anything.

She begged her mother.

Mrs. Young realized that her daughter was serious, but knew they couldn't afford the trip. Although she didn't think Brittany would be able to do it in such a short time, Mrs. Young told her: "If you can raise the money, you can go."

Brittany never backed down from a challenge. She estimated that she would need about $3,000 to go on the trip. She only had a few months to raise the money. Brittany started by babysitting every chance she got. But after a month or so, she realized she wouldn't earn enough that way. For the next week, she wondered what to do.

The answer came to her as she stood in her kitchen, pulling a pie from the oven. "Mom, do you think anyone would buy my pies if I sold them?"

Mrs. Young loved her daughter's pies, and was sure that they would sell. But to make $3,000, Brittany would have to sell an impossible number of pies. "I'm sure they would," she answered. "I don't know if you'd be able to . . ."

"I think I can," Brittany said, before her mother could finish her sentence.

Within weeks, family and friends were enjoying Brittany's homemade fruit pies. After school, she baked three or four a night! When Brittany sold her final pie, a few months later, she had raised $4,000! This was $1,000 more than she needed for her trip.

Unfortunately, Spain never happened. Shortly

before they were supposed to leave, there was a terrorist bombing in Morocco. Brittany's parents decided it wasn't safe for Brittany to travel abroad. So she put her "pie" money away and hoped for another trip.

She didn't have to wait long. At the end of her freshman year, Coach Rudy decided to take some runners to Baltimore, Maryland. They would be racing against some of the best runners on the east coast. Brittany was thrilled. She had never been to Maryland and was excited to compete. To visit someplace new, and face new competition, would be a great challenge.

Brittany and her friend Erin at the Capitol Building in Washington DC.

When they arrived in Washington DC, the girls took some time to sightsee. They only had one day to see the city. The following day they would head thirty miles away to Baltimore. Although it rained, nothing slowed them down. They toured the Washington Monument, the White House, the Lincoln Memorial, the Jefferson Memorial, the United States Holocaust Memorial Museum, and as much of the Smithsonian as they could.

Brittany loved taking hikes in the beautiful surroundings of Maui. As a nature lover, she didn't realize how much she would enjoy her "city hike." It was like nothing she had experienced. Washington DC was different from her small island, but she couldn't get enough of it.

Brittany was excited to share her experience with friends and family. She couldn't wait to tell them that she'd seen the White House! Brittany and her friend, Erin, still laugh about the aggressive "spy" squirrels. One of these furry creatures actually bit her butt as she sat on the wall.

One of the "spy" squirrels at the White House.

These experiences almost made Brittany forget why she'd come to Maryland in the first place: to run. The next day came quickly. When the girls arrived at the track, they were intimidated. They noticed expensive running shoes, sleek windbreakers, and sponsorship tents. This was a "big time" track event.

Most of her teammates whispered to one another nervously. Brittany tried to stay focused. Still, she was anxious about how she would fare against these talented runners. It was one thing to be the best on Maui. Brittany knew that her times needed to be faster to compete nationally.

Brittany ran the four hundred meter race first. She was shocked by the speed of the other girls. She didn't even make it to the finals. In Maui, she always made the finals. Although she was disappointed, she put it behind her. She would have to make up for it in the eight hundred meter race. In this race, she planned to use her regular strategy: *stay behind the leaders until the last two hundred meters, then start your kick, and out-sprint them to the finish line.*

That is not how things went. Brittany started out just behind the leaders, as she had planned. But when she was about to make her move, she found herself trapped in a tight pack. She couldn't cut the corner. The pace was fast, but Brittany knew that she could run faster—if only she could break out. She had never raced in such a large group. Getting bumped around by older and stronger runners was no fun.

The race was more than half over. Brittany tried to force her body forward on the inside. Just as she passed a few girls, she was nudged hard. She fell into the metal edge that bordered the infield. She barely managed to get back up and finish the race.

Overall, it was a disappointing day. There was a valuable lesson, though. The physical style of these east coast runners was something Brittany would have to get used to. Especially if she planned on running in bigger meets. The runners in Maui were often passive. She hadn't realized that until she ran in Baltimore.

When she boarded the flight back to Maui, she knew that she'd be back. This was only the beginning.

Back home in Maui, Brittany sits on the track bleachers and reflects on her race in DC.

Chapter Six

Too Much

When Brittany's sophomore year began, Tia started college on the mainland. This meant that there were no runners left on Brittany's team to really push her. After the meet in Baltimore, she knew her running needed some work. That's why she started training with a different team: the boy's team.

Hanging out with boys all the time wasn't as fun as hanging out with the girls. Running with them was great, though. Brittany welcomed the challenge. She loved to train—the harder, the better.

Cross country training is intense. There are daily twenty to sixty-minute runs, as well as weightlifting three times each week. Still, Brittany wanted more. In addition to practices, she would get up at five thirty in the morning to run before school.

The extra training paid off. Brittany had an

excellent sophomore season. She took first place in almost all of her races. She ended the season as the Maui Interscholastic League champion. This was rare for a sophomore. She was also, once again, on her way to the state meet. It was being held on the Big Island. Traveling there brought back memories of flying with her mother to get her legs checked. For some, these memories would be painful, but Brittany cherished them. Her injury was a reminder of her strength.

Sophomore year: Brittany and her cross country teammates.

At the state cross country meet, Brittany started out with the pack. Soon, the need to sprint took over and she started to pull away. She was in a zone, and had no idea how many girls she had passed. There were more than 185 runners, so it was hard to tell.

When she crossed the finish line, she was excited. She thought she had placed around tenth place. Her actual place wouldn't be revealed until the awards ceremony.

Brittany was confused as the names were announced for the top twenty runners. *Why aren't they calling me?* she wondered. Just as this thought entered her mind, the announcer said, "In fourth place, from Seabury Hall…"

Brittany never actually heard him say her name. The shrieks from her teammates drowned out the loudspeaker. Brittany was excited. She had hoped to do well, but fourth place was amazing. After all, 185 of the best runners in the state were competing. It was a far cry from last year, when she was ninety-seventh!

Brittany had been running both cross country and track for years. Truthfully, she had always preferred track. With this recent success, though, things were changing. She was discovering that she might have an equal passion for cross country.

When cross country ended, Coach Rudy advised against Brittany playing soccer. He was afraid she would get hurt. Instead, he recommended paddling. This sport was fun and would help develop Brittany's upper body strength. Paddling is a big sport in Hawaii. It requires strength and stamina, as well as determination. The ocean can be unforgiving at times. There are many days when paddlers have to face dangerous conditions. That was just what Brittany wanted—an adventure.

During her first season, Brittany was moved up to varsity and given the position of stroker. There are six girls in the outrigger canoe: one steersman and five paddlers. The paddler in the front is called the stroker. This person sets the pace for the boat. That person was Brittany. She had strength, stamina, and was used to pushing through pain. Plus, she never gave up.

Brittany and the Seabury paddling team.

The team trained at the Kahului Harbor on the North Shore. Brittany loved being on the water with friends. She enjoyed feeling the salt air on her skin. Just as in running, she loved pushing her body to the limit. She found the regattas (races) fun, but also extremely challenging.

High school regattas are a half mile long. There

are usually about six canoes positioned next to their colored flag. The starter, who is up ahead in a motor boat, gives the final command. Then the teams take off. They race a quarter mile out, and go around their colored flag. The quarter mile race back to their starting position is always the most exciting.

The Seabury team had a great season and qualified for the state meet in Waikiki on Oahu. Brittany was excited to go, but she had a problem. The state regatta was the same day as her first track meet of the season! The two events were on different islands, so she couldn't do both. It was decided that she would go to the regatta on Oahu. Then she would jump into the track season. Although both of her coaches agreed on this, Coach Rudy was concerned. He though Brittany might be wearing herself out.

She started the track season a week late. On any given day she would do as many as twelve four-hundred meter runs. She also did weight training three times per week. Her training paid off at the MIL time trials in April. She won the four hundred meter dash in a time of 59:12 seconds. This time was just shy of breaking her record. It was fast enough to make her the number one seed for the MIL Championship meet.

She ran well in the four hundred meter dash two days later. Unfortunately, she lost the MIL Championship in a photo finish to her good friend Erin Wooldridge. They had competed against each other for years. They were tough competitors from rival schools. Despite this, it was common to see them hugging and joking before the start of a race. Even though she lost, Brittany was happy for Erin.

Erin and Brittany share a hug shortly after competing against one another.

There was a silver lining later that day. Brittany bounced back to win first place in the eight hundred meter dash. For the third time this year, Brittany was on her way to a state championship.

The state meet was around the corner and Brittany was wearing down. She always felt tired. Going to school, fulfilling her committee obligations, running every afternoon (and often in the morning as well), then studying until late into the night, was simply too much. Plus, Brittany was also involved in a community service project called Dancing Palette. This program took up two hours every Sunday, which was her only day off.

Dancing Palette was started by a girl at Seabury Hall who had a handicapped brother. The program helps young children with disabilities. Brittany's memories of the children she'd met at The Shriners Hospitals for Children made it easy for her to relate. Brittany's role in Dancing Palette was to organize activities. There were crafts, baking, music programs, and games. She was also responsible for fundraising.

Her hectic schedule finally caught up to her. Brittany had never recovered from paddling season two months earlier. By the time the state track meet came around in April, Brittany felt terrible—and it showed. She was winded and weak. She still managed to place fifth in the four hundred meter dash. But she took a disappointing eighth place in the eight hundred.

The running world still recognized Brittany's talents. In cross country, she was voted the Maui Interscholastic League Female Runner of the Year. In track, she made the All-Star Team (top runner in each running event at the MIL Finals) for the eight hundred meter run. She also received an Honorable Mention for the four hundred meter dash. In her greatest honor, she was named the Seabury Hall Female Athlete of the Year. This award was usually reserved for seniors.

These achievements were great. But Brittany was ignoring the signals her body was giving her. She needed a break.

Brittany trains on the track at King Keaulike High School.

Chapter Seven

No More Changes!

The summer before her junior year, Brittany trained with the track club. Preparing for the fall season was actually fun for Brittany. She had run last summer, too. It had been cool because Jake and Makenna had run. Although they were not running this summer, Brittany hung out with them a lot.

The track club was fun because Brittany's friends were running. There was Erin, as well as Brittany Feiteira. These three girls were known as The Three Compadres. They were inseparable.

Brittany's summer was going great until her father made a shocking announcement: "We sold the house." As the words left his lips, everyone was stunned. Although they knew the day was coming, it still didn't seem real. Mr. and Mrs. Young had put the house up for sale, and then off the market again, many times. They were never sure if they wanted to sell it. In the meantime, Brittany had become attached to her home.

Brittany had lived there since she was two weeks old. She spent most of her childhood exploring every square inch of the wooded property. And then there was Jackie, Brittany's neighbor and friend since the day she'd moved there. Although their new home was only a town away, it didn't seem right leaving Jackie behind.

Brittany sat on the floor of her bedroom, boxing up everything that belonged to her. She thought about all her wonderful memories of home. There were hundred of hours spent sitting on the window seat in her bedroom, thinking. Sometimes at night, she would lie awake in her bed. She'd watch the moon glide across the sky as she ran the next day's race in her head.

There were other memories, too: the road . . . the protea farm . . . the burn pit . . . the run home . . . Brittany recalled it all as if it had happened yesterday. She had no desire to leave any of it behind. In the end, she had no choice. The house was sold. She sadly finished taping up the boxes and glanced out the window one last time.

Shortly after moving, Brittany and five other girls went with Coach Rudy to California. They were participating in the Pacific Association Junior Olympic Track and Field Championships. Brittany always enjoyed running out of state. Plus, her friend Erin was one of the girls going.

The five girls had a blast. They also made an impressive showing. Brittany took first place in the eight hundred, setting a personal record of 2:17 minutes. She also took second place in the fifteen hundred, and fourth place in the four hundred. In addition, the girls teamed up for a second place finish in the 4x400 meter relay. Brittany's success in California was a great way to bounce back from last season's disappointing finish.

When she returned to school in the fall, Coach Rudy was gone. He was no longer at Seabury Hall. This was a major disappointment for Brittany. The junior year is the most important year for an athlete in search of a college scholarship. This is the year when colleges begin deciding who to offer scholarships to. Brittany knew this, which made her twice as nervous about Coach Rudy leaving.

Life was changing and Brittany was stressed. This weighed heavily on her as the cross country season started. Luckily, her new coach Tom Rehrer was a familiar face. Tom had been a coach at Seabury for several years. This was great, because Brittany knew him well. Still, it would be an adjustment.

Brittany with her new coach, Tom Rehrer.

Mentally, Brittany went into her junior season with a good attitude. But despite her winning races, her body was wearing down. In fact, she was having trouble breathing. At first, she tried to brush it off. She trained harder to make up for her lack of energy. This strategy worked for a while, but only a short while.

Once again, Brittany qualified for the state cross country meet. She was also named the MIL Runner of the Year, again. But her health was getting worse. She finally got medical attention. A doctor told her that she might have exercise induced asthma. That is a breathing disorder that develops when your body is under physical stress. Because of this, Brittany was given an inhaler to use before she ran. Although it helped, she didn't have her full strength back.

The cross country state meet in the fall of 2005 didn't go well. Brittany got caught up in the pre-race excitement and forgot to use her inhaler. She started the race strong, only to fade. With a half mile behind her, Brittany started having trouble breathing. Her lungs felt like they were going to explode.

For the first time in her life, she didn't know whether she could finish the race. But Brittany was a fighter. She struggled through the three miles and finished in fifty-fifth place. This was a disappointing end to her cross country season.

When the team returned to Maui, a yearbook reporter asked Brittany about her proudest moment of the season. He was expecting her to talk about one of her many great races. But Brittany answered, "Definitely the state meet. I ran the worst race of my life, but I finished, and all my girls ran their best races, and fastest times all season. I was super stoked for them."

Brittany's love for her teammates is mutual. In fact, her cross country team voted Brittany the captain during her junior season.

The track season started in the spring, and Brittany had everybody psyched. She calmed their nerves too. Sure, with a new coach, there were certainly going to be some changes. Brittany felt good about them, though.

Tom Rehrer is a long distance coach, which was great for Brittany. Recently, she'd had great success in the eight hundred—a long distance race. In playing to both their strengths, Coach Rehrer decided to have Brittany concentrate on longer races. He was confident that Brittany could win the state meet in the eight hundred. He wanted to pace her so she wouldn't burn herself out. Being a state champion was a big goal. It was one that Brittany felt she could accomplish, though.

Coach Tom worked hard to help Brittany relax. Brittany expected more from herself than anybody else. Sometimes this worked against her. Coach Tom wasn't convinced that Brittany had exercise induced asthma, either. He thought that she had simply overtrained. He insisted that she was participating in too many activities. This season, Coach Tom made sure Brittany was more careful with her schedule. He wanted her to take time to relax her body and mind.

Brittany spends a lot of her free time hiking or hanging out by the water. These activities help to relax her body and mind.

Brittany still practiced hard, but she enjoyed it more now. Seeing Brittany sprinting around the track long after others have left is a common sight. Her beautiful running form is highlighted by long, powerful strides.

Brittany won easily during the first track meet of the spring season. She ran a 2:19 for the eight hundred and felt strong doing it. She did not have any trouble breathing either. It seemed as though she had cleared that hurdle.

After that race, Brittany officially decided to focus on the eight hundred, fifteen hundred, and the three thousand. Sure, she wanted to run the shorter races and the relays like she used to. But he training was now geared to focus on longer events. This new program worked very well. In fact, she raced that entire season without losing!

The state track meet came up on May 13, 2006. Brittany, with the help of Coach Tom, was ready. This was her biggest chance to shine. College scouts would definitely be interested in the outcome of this race.

Brittany wore a focused expression at the starting line. She was trying to be the best eight hundred meter runner in the state. Seeded number one, she was on the rail.

"Runners take your mark!" The eight elite runners shifted into their favorite starting stances. They would stay in their lanes for a hundred meters, and then cut to the post.

"Get Set!" Everyone breathed in at once.

"BANG!" The starting gun exploded as the biggest race of Brittany's life began.

Chapter Eight

Born to Run

The runners took off. They stayed mostly together as they hit the one hundred meter mark. As usual, Brittany's strategy was on the shoulder of the lead runner. Then, at the last two hundred meters, she would shift into another gear. She and Coach Tom had researched all the runners. They felt confident about their strategy.

After the first hundred meters, Brittany was bunched in with the other runners, slightly behind the leader. At the two hundred mark, she moved out into lane four to get around the pack. This added some distance to the run. But Brittany knew it was the only way to get up front.

She passed everyone but the lead runner, then settled into her stride. The two girls started to pull away from the group. By the four hundred mark, they were significantly ahead.

"Sixty-seven!" The official called out the split time for the first lap. Brittany was three seconds off her pace. Her goal was to run the race in 2:15 or less. She had run sixty-four second laps at practice. Although she was behind her time, she knew she had to remain patient. These were the best runners in the state. If she accelerated too soon, she might be out-sprinted in the end. Running the race in 2:15 would be nice, but her first priority was to win. So she held back and stuck to her plan.

Brittany planned to start her sprint during the last two hundred meters, but her adrenaline kicked in early. With three hundred meters to go, she took off. The question now was: could she keep it up to the finish line? The lead runner did not keep pace. The runners in third and fourth quickly closed the gap on her. She could hear their feet pounding behind her. Her only chance at victory was to sprint all the way to the finish line.

They headed into the final curve. Brittany sprinted for the line. The screaming from the stands made her think the runners were on her heels! She pushed harder.

In the end, Brittany crossed the finish line a full second ahead of the second place finisher. She was the new state champion in the eight hundred meter run!

Brittany was thrilled. Her time of 2:19:08, though, was not as fast as she had hoped. She believes that she can reduce her eight hundred time to compete nationally. Brittany has already set high running goals for her senior year. She dreams of running competitively in college, too.

The biggest obstacle Brittany faces in realizing her dreams is her love of doing *everything*. Coach Tom knows that Brittany has not yet reached her full potential in running. He claims that the main reason she won the state meet was because she focused on one event. He is constantly telling Brittany that she needs to prioritize—and not be involved in so many things. He believes that if she focuses on the eight hundred meter run, her potential is limitless. Right now, though, she's having too much fun to be so serious.

In an interview that focused on Brittany, Coach Tom said, "Brittany likes a lot of things: art, all different sports, social activities, and she's got a lot of friends—she's a typical sixteen-year-old girl. But at some level I think she's probably fighting with herself, kind of asking, 'Do I want to give up some of this stuff to pursue it for real.'"

Brittany may not be ready to prioritize her interests yet, but she is definitely motivated. Her fellow students voted her as their student body president for her senior year. Knowing Brittany, it will be another active year. Brittany has no plans of slowing down. She has big dreams for the future—on and off the track. Beyond college plans, Brittany wants to organize a 10 K run to support The Shriners Hospitals for Children. She is appreciative of the care she received there, and would like to give something back.

In May, 2006, Brittany spoke in front of her entire high school. It was for her speech class, and had to be about a life-altering experience. Brittany once again risked being made fun of as she stood at the podium. Four hundred pairs of eyes were focused on her, waiting for her to tell a story—a story that few had heard.

Brittany knew that she had a reputation in school. She was known for her athletic talent and probably her bubbly personality, too. Yet, some students misunderstood her. They thought she was obsessive about her workouts. Some thought that she was a little too enthusiastic about life in general. Today, she would explain why.

Brittany took a deep breath. She pushed the memory of the third grader who thought her legs were "gross" from her mind. She knew that in speaking about her accident, she was risking this type of reaction again. Things were different this time, though. The scars were still there, but they were not gross to Brittany. She had grown to see them in a positive light, a reminder that she was lucky to be standing at this podium—lucky to be standing at all.

Brittany looked out at the crowd and took a deep breath. Then she told them about the burn pit, her run up the hill on Cooke Road, her scarred feet, her fears, and her seven-year recovery. She talked about the sick and burned children she had come to know, and how they affected her life. She talked about the life lessons she learned along the way.

"Along my journey to healing I was exposed to so many other children, older and younger, with medical problems far worse than my own. Once you think you have a 'bad' situation you need to step out of the box of self-absorption and realize how lucky you really are. There is always, and I can guarantee always, someone else out there with far worse of a 'bad' situation."

Everyone was visibly moved as she described the details of her journey. Brittany ended her speech with a famous quote, answering the most often asked question: Why do you run?

"John F. Kennedy once said, 'As we express our gratitude, we must never forget that the highest appreciation is not to utter words, but to live by them.' I not only learned the typical lesson, don't take every moment—or should I say, step you take for granted.

But I also realized that you must always take action upon what you say you learn. For the past several years I have often been questioned why I run. Now you know. It is not genetics, it's determination. Determination to show how appreciative I am that I was given the ability to heal. Running is not a pain, it's a privilege. Every step I take when I walk, every stride I take when I run, I embrace what I have because I never know when all that I have could be gone."

Brittany still bears scars on her feet, but she is thankful for every step she takes. Brittany's heart is as big as her incredible talent. She was born to win races, born to inspire people—but more than anything, she was born to run.